DROPSHIPPING

Complete Step-by-Step Guide for Beginners to Create a Profitable Shopify Dropshipping Store from Scratch and Make Money online from Home

2020-2021 Edition

Brian Corey

©**Copyright 2020** All rights reserved

All rights reserved. No part of this publication may be reproduced, redistributed or transmitted in any form or by any means, including photocopying, recording, or other electronic or mechanical methods, without the prior written permission of the publisher, except in the case of brief quotations, embodied in critical reviews and certain other non-commercial uses permitted by copyright law.

Disclaimer:

This book is for educational purposes only. There is no guarantee that you will earn any money using the techniques and ideas mentioned in this book. This is not financial advice. Your level of success in attaining the results claimed in this book will require hard-work, experience, and knowledge. We have taken reasonable steps to ensure that the information on this book is accurate, but we cannot represent that the website(s) mentioned in this book are free from errors. You expressly agree not to rely upon any information contained in this book.

Covered image "Designed by Freepik"

Table of Contents

Introduction 1

Chapter 1 7

Introduction To Dropshipping 7

Chapter 2 21

How To Find The Perfect Product For Your Store 21

Chapter 3 29

Product Research Techniques 29

Chapter 4 41

How To Find A Great Dropshipping Supplier 41

Chapter 5 57

Setting Up Your Shopify Store 57

Chapter 6 78

The Absolute Best Apps To Use For Your Store 78

Chapter 7 87

Marketing Your Dropshipping Business
.... 87

Chapter 8 109

How To Handle Refunds, Returns & Replacements For Dropshipped Products 109

Final Tips For Long Term Success 124

Resources 131

About The Author 132

Introduction

Thank you for purchasing this book. In this book, I'll be teaching how to create, design, and build a profitable Dropshipping store from scratch for complete beginners. Now, if you just found out about dropshipping, that's awesome! it's an amazing business model especially if you are just starting out with online business and with e-commerce, and if you've been wanting to build your own Shopify store and start an online passive income business, this book is the perfect book for you because in this book, I'm going to be giving you information that will literally cost you cost $4,000 $5,000 to obtained somewhere else, I'm going to give it all to you without holding anything back.

This book is designed to be a complete A-to-Z, 0 to 100 entire step-by-step tutorial, including how to design your store, running Facebook ads, running Instagram ads, and the best sources of traffic. Why do I have to write this particular book? The truth is there's a lot of books and courses out there, and some of them are really great courses. But the thing is that they're all old, they're all from 2017-2018. I've been in e-commerce for a few years now and trust me, since I started, things have changed a lot. Things change every single day, every single month, and that's why I'm happy to be presenting this book to you today because it's fully up to date and it has the best strategy to succeed, the fastest possible way so you can go quit your 9-to-5 job forever and replace it with a profitable online business with Shopify dropshipping.

I'm also tired of other books teaching you how to build dropshipping stores using just Oberlo and Aliexpress, copying products from Aliexpress and using an app called Oberlo just to paste it on a store. Now this may have worked in 2017 or 2018, trust me this doesn't work anymore! I tried it myself when I first got it to dropshipping and let me tell you, it's just the short-term way of doing things. If you want to truly have success in your life, the only way to do it is by focusing on the long term, and this book is going to be showing you how to actually build a long-term business with Shopify where it's going to be putting money in your pocket every single month for years to come, and something that you'll have as an asset that you can later on maybe pass down to your kids or sell later for an actual price that is in millions of dollars.

I will be showing you my strategy that I personally developed and personally use on my stores and stores that I've taken to eight figures per year which is ten million dollars per year which is fully possible. This isn't something crazy in e-commerce especially when you're selling something at $50 or $100 per unit, you can see that it doesn't take all that many units to actually get to those numbers. This is called branded dropshipping. I believed branded dropshipping is the future and trust me I've done millions of dollars in online sales.

Branded dropshipping is the future because you're actually building a brand, you're taking a product and you're building an actual brand out of it with complimentary products. If you look at any successful e-commerce store out there, it's a branded store, and they probably start off as dropshipping.

If you're not too familiar with the business model, dropshipping is a really amazing for a beginner, for someone starting out because there's literally no risk when you're starting out. The only things you have to pay for is the Shopify plan. You get a free trial for the first 14 days and then $29 a month. And then you might have to pay for the domain name, that's $10 or $20, and that's pretty much it. I mean there's not really much else that you have to pay for with dropshipping. And the beautiful part about dropshipping is that you don't take any inventory risk that you're taking with something like Amazon or something else.

At the beginning with the dropshipping you can test out if a product is good, you can build a branded dropshipping store, and you don't even have to order any units! You don't have to order 100 or 1000 units. There are lots of suppliers out there that will dropship for you with your logo and they'll do it very well. They'll do it with good packaging, with good branding design that you'll create. I'll show you how to do that as well and so that way you're not taking any risk on inventory.

Chapter 1

Introduction to Dropshipping

Dropshipping is a business model where store owners can sell products without actually creating, manufacturing, or stocking the products themselves. It is an ecommerce business where you can run a store without stocking any product physically. Once you get an order, your supplier will shipped the items from their factory or warehouse to your customer. You don't have to worry about packaging, storing, or delivering the product yourself

Let's say someone pays $200 for a product on your store, and you pay your supplier $50 for the product, and you spent $10 for ads to acquire the customer, $140 is your profit.

In summary, this is how dropshipping works:

1. The customer places an order for a product on the retailer's online store.

2. The retailer automatically or manually forwards the order and customer details to the dropship supplier.

3. The dropship supplier packages and ships the order directly to the customer in the retailer's name

Why does this model work so well and why is it so popular

Historically, there have been three big challenges for people who want to run their own store. First and foremost, when it comes to running your ecommerce business, you need a store, you need a place to sell stuff. Then the internet came and Shopify came along and now anyone can open a store in a matter of hours, or even minutes! Store no longer means what it used to, you don't need brick-and-mortar, you don't need a spot inside of a mall, but you can definitely open a store for free no problem, so the stores challenge of having a place to sell your products has been solved with dropshipping.

Then there's the marketing challenge, and the idea here is that once you have a store, you still need to make sure people know about it, you need to make noise about your store because if people don't know your store exists, it's going to be a slog selling anything. The marketing challenge is another one that's been addressed by modern tech which has reduced the barrier to entry to just about nothing when it comes to marketing. Think about it, Facebook gives you a platform to market its over 2 billion users, Google AdWords allows you to reach people who are looking for the exact words that you want them to be looking for when they find your store and so on. There's a lot of places that you can market, problem solved!

That leaves us with the products. You can have a great store, and great marketing strategies, have all your ads figured out. But if you don't have good products you're going to have problems and this is where dropshipping comes. When you dropship, your suppliers have the products, not you, they've taken care of the product part, that leaves you to just create the store, to make it pretty, to market your products; products that you don't have to manufacture or don't have to keep in a warehouse somewhere. Not having to hold your own inventory is such a game-changer for people who want to launch their own businesses, it's a cost saver, it's a space saver, and it makes it so convenient to launch your own store.

Benefits of Dropshipping Business

As a business model, there are several attributes of dropshipping which has proven the business as a beneficial one, some of these benefits include:

1. Easy to start

It doesn't take an entire village to set up since it essentially involves just 3 steps—find the supplier, set up your website and start selling the goods! To someone who is new to the ecommerce industry, this business model is relatively easy to understand and implement. You don't have to store products you don't have to invest in inventory and you don't have to have a physical store to make your sales.

2. Dropshipping is flexible:

Another big benefit of dropshipping is that it's flexible. If you want to ramp up a business at your own pace, dropshipping is a great way to do that. You can run the business at your own pace without feeling pressure to make sales immediately to pay rent. You can tap into suppliers, get photos of their products to learn about their products and then to see which products works best with the different target groups that you wanted to market to.

This is something that you can do before you go to work, or on the weekends when you get home if it's not a full-time thing, that's no problem, you can have success at your own pace and do things without feeling a bunch of pressure to make a ton of sales

Another aspect of this flexibility is the products themselves. Because you don't have inventory you can test, you're not committed to a supplier there's no contractual agreement that when you make a Facebook ad with their product, that you're going to be committed to buying and selling a certain amount of that product. So if you find that you're not making sales with a certain product or with a certain set of products you can just move on, no problem.

3. Low start-up capital

You can start a dropshipping store especially at the beginning without investing a bunch of money. To be honest, it does cost a little bit of money. So when you hear about making a million dollars without investing anything, it's not exactly true. That said, what you do need to invest is minimal, you need to buy a Shopify subscription, you might need to install an app or two on your website, and then you're going to need to test products that you want to sell to ensure the reliability of the supplier to check out the packaging and the shipping time, we're talking about a couple hundred bucks. But again, this is nothing compared to the investment that it would take to start a company say 15 or 20 years ago. You can get up and running with just a few hundred bucks.

4. **Easy to Manage**

Dropshipping stores are easy to manage, especially compared to traditional business models. Think about it, once you have your store set up, and you established contact with the suppliers, then a lot of this is just going to be on autopilot. Shopify is going to take care of the store part, the supplier is going to take care of the product part, and then it's on you to simply market and ensure that people know about your products and ensure that they're satisfied once they get the products. That's not to say it's easy, there's a lot of time and energy that's going to be required to start and to scale and to grow a dropshipping store. But the point is, it's easier to manage than say trying to order something from a different country and then finding someplace to store it, and then getting rid of inventory that is cluttering up your warehouse, or worse yet, your living room.

Compared to that, dropshipping is super simple and the store and the marketing become your focal point not, the products. There will be some investments on your end, especially finding the right products at the beginning but once you do, it's really easy to manage.

5. Scalable

Dropshipping is super scalable. Your costs aren't going to get out of control as you grow. You're not going to be required to get more warehouse space, you're not going to be required to build more storefronts, and you're not going to be required to hold more inventory of different types of products. That is non-existent in the dropshipping business model. Scaling is going to be more based on marketing and the diversity of products that you offer. So if you go from a two product store, to a five product store, to a ten product store. It's not as though all those products need to be lying around waiting for orders. You can and offer these without having to invest heavily in them. The real monetary investment when it comes to scaling is going to be on the marketing side, Shopify is going to take care of your store, your suppliers are going to take care of the products, that leaves just the marketing aspect to you. And by the time you get to the this scaling portion of your dropshipping journey you've already known what works, you've already known what types of ads, what types of products, what types of offers generate the most buzz.

Common Dropshipping questions

So before we go further, I want to answer some common questions that you might have before starting dropshipping

Question 1

Can I do this from anywhere in the world?

Ans: Yes you can! It doesn't matter where you are in the world. Today there are so many opportunities for people out there to change their lives with online business, with dropshipping and with e-commerce. Right now we're undergoing the craziest transformation in history and e-commerce will be huge, it's going to be 100 times bigger than what it is now, that's why I'm so happy that you're here reading this book and you're learning the right information for you to set yourself up for success.

Question 2

How much money do I need to start?

Ans: You can start with as little as 200 or $300. If you have like literally 50 to 100 dollars, then that might be too low. But if you have 200 or 300 dollars or at least have access to that, then that's enough money for you to start. The great part about dropshipping is that you really don't need a lot of money because you don't have to order a lot of units upfront, that's why if you have only a few hundred dollars, then that's enough for you to actually get your store up and running. And the most important part is taking action. If you can start taking action today you'll see that your circumstances today will line up in a way where you will succeed. Most people don't take any action and that's exactly why they fail because they don't even try. So if you try and you actually follow every single step that I will outlined in this book, then the chances of you succeeding are very high. So if you have about 200-300 dollars that's enough. If you have $500 or more, let's say $500 to $1000, that's even better because then you can start running Facebook ads. At that budget you can really make your store take off much faster. Advertisements is the key to making your store grow like a wildfire and I'm going to talk about that as well.

Question 3

Can't my customers just go on AliExpress and buy it themselves?

Ans: Yes they can, but they won't! There's a reason why there's so many successful brands out there. All the products are made in China, they all can be found on Aliexpress but people still want to buy the product in stores, or online on their online stores, not from Aliexpress, Why? Because people want quality, and quality only comes if you build a brand, and that's why branded dropshipping is the way to go. It is the true way to win on Shopify.

Chapter 2

How to find the perfect Product for your Store

In this chapter, I will be showing you how to find the perfect product for you to start your dropshipping store.

To consider a product good enough or perfect for your store, the product must meet the following criteria:

1. **The product must have a WOW factor**

Your product must have a WOW factor to be regarded as a perfect product for your store. Getting a product with this attributes entails applying the best methods into researching your products. There are many methods you can use when it comes to product research, and for me, I actually only used two and just from these two techniques that I'm going to show you, I found products that have personally made me hundreds of thousands of dollars per month in sales. It doesn't have to be complicated and it's not hard to make money, it really isn't. It's just a simple step-by-step process, you just have to follow something that is already working for someone, and in this case it's clearly working for me and for many other sellers out there.

2. The Product must be of high quality and of great/ new design

Having a high quality product is essential to your overall success in dropshipping business. Let's say you are able to find a product on Aliexpress or Alibaba (and we're going to talk about finding products on Alibaba that is literally my hidden secret).

If you can find the product out there but the quality isn't great, then you'll see that your store is going to be always hindered, it's always going to be not as good as it can be because your product isn't that great. So the number one thing is to have and find a great product the better your product is, the better the quality is, and then the better you're setting yourself up for faster and more success from the very beginning

3. The product can be found on Alibaba or AliExpress

You must be able to actually find the product on Aliexpress or Alibaba. Now, AliExpress and Alibaba are two different websites. AliExpress is basically what the most common dropshipping website, it is the website that all the courses and books out there are teaching you to go and just copy and paste products from there. And because of that, it has become the most competitive website and it's filled with middleman, it's filled with not even factories, it is filled with just ordinary people in China who know the system, who played the system, and who take advantage of the fact that there are so many people who want to start dropshipping, and they're following outdated information. So they're getting crazy expensive prices and extremely unreliable shipping. And so it's just a broken system, it doesn't work.

I recommend that you don't source your product from AliExpress, but your product must be found on Aliexpress or Alibaba. I prefer using Alibaba because I thought to myself, the suppliers on Aliexpress and Alibaba are probably not that different, and they're probably the same suppliers, except they're just charging more money on

Aliexpress. What if I go and I send out my supplier template on Alibaba to the suppliers and I just asked them a couple of dropshipping related questions? Like can you drop ship this for me? Can you put a logo on this? And it worked great. And most of my successful products with dropshipping have come from Alibaba Suppliers, and the suppliers down there are just so much better because they're used to professional relationships they're used to huge numbers, that's why they really want to make something work with you even if you're someone who's starting out.

4. **The Product must be in a passionate niche and or target market**

The last and final point here that you need to find a great product in a passionate niche or targeted market. It's always better if your product really is in a passionate niche or target market because if your product is in a passionate niche for example, like camping, hiking, or fishing, or beauty or let's say sustainable beauty or, or veganism, obviously people are very passionate about these things and the more you can niche down, the better. But you also don't want to really niche down too much because then you're not going to have as many people that would be interested in your product. To be honest with you, I would either go with something that's super broad, a product that can be used by many people out there, or something that is in a more passionate niche, something that is more niched down. And that way, it's just easier to target on Facebook.

Best Niches for Dropshipping

Before we get to the first product research technique that I'm going to show you I want to talk about the list of the best niches for dropshipping. There are so many niches, there aren't any particular niches that are way better than others. Some of the best niches include:

1. Luxury accessories
2. Camping
3. Hiking
4. Survival
5. Gardening
6. Eco-Friendly Products
7. Golf
8. Tennis
9. Football/Soccer
10. Cooking/ kitchen
11. Outdoor Patio/ Lawn/ Garden
12. Beauty

13. Jewelry
14. Clothing (niche down)
15. Automotive Accessories

All these niches are very profitable and great place to start, you could find products for any of these. You don't have to find something that you're passionate about, that's a huge misconception, just find something that works. Find something where you can see that the product fits the criteria that we talked about; has a WOW factor, has a great quality, and it can be found on Alibaba or Aliexpress and also has a passion niche; has people in the niche that are really passionate about their products and are willing to spend money for them.

Chapter 3

Product Research Techniques

Product research is one of the most important aspect that you need to get right if you would be successful in dropshipping. Many courses out there usually talk about getting all these special kinds of tools that cost you a lot of money, and for someone who's starting out, that's obviously very difficult because you're on a limited budget. Most people nowadays who are starting are on a limited budget because they got their 9-5 job, and they're probably paying bills, and so they only got some extra cash to put aside to start their online business. I totally understand, and that's why I'm going to show you my favorite product research technique that doesn't involve having 20 different tools.

Now it might be surprising, but one of the best ways I've found to actually find profitable dropshipping products is just to go on social media like on Facebook and scroll down on the feeds, and I'm telling you, I found a lot of amazing products. For example right here we can see its some kind a watch store

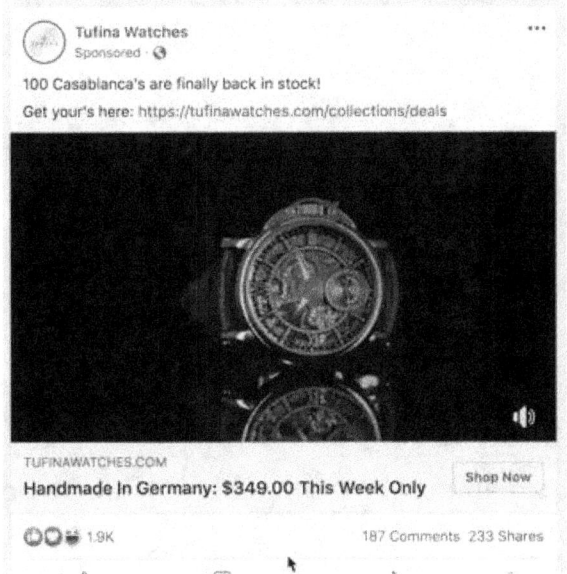

On first glance you might think "okay well it looks like a nice watch, probably not dropshipping, it doesn't look cheap, it looks high-quality." And literally look it's just an ad of them showing the watch, there's not really any brand it looks like. If we go on their store you can very easily tell that it is a Shopify store.

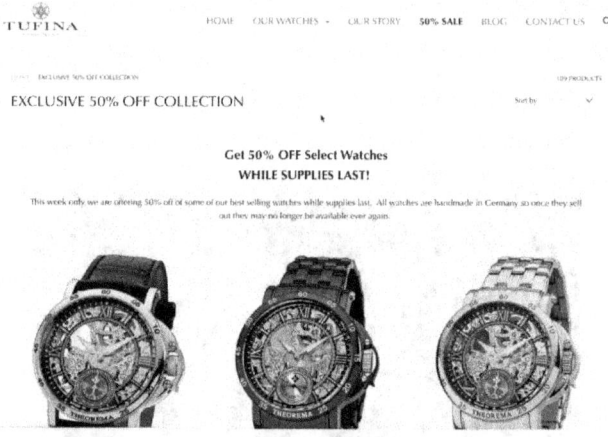

We can see they're selling for $367 Canadian dollars so not cheap. If we go on Alibaba and we try finding this watch we would just go type in "luxury watch leather leather wristband"

You can see watches for $5 to $15 dollars, $20, $50 and so on, and for someone who has an eye for style, this could be a great opportunity. You might think watches are incredibly competitive, but this store alone is making a kill selling these watches.

Alexa Traffic rank

We use an app called Alexa traffic rank to know how much money a dropshipping store is making, it's a free app that you can install that tells you how much money a dropshipping store is making. But doesn't tell you that in dollars, it tells you that in traffic rank. It is a free app, just go to Google and type in Alexa Site rank Google Chrome extension.

I will show you how to interpret that right now.

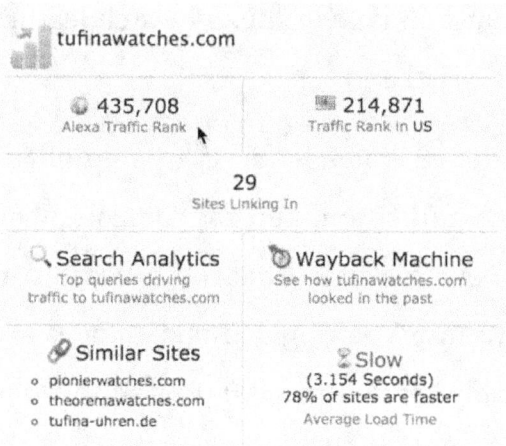

If we go back to the store there are 214, 871 traffic rank in the US and 435,708 worldwide. Alexa scans and ranks every single website based on the amount of traffic going in, and traffic is basically the amount of people that are visiting the website every day. Therefore, for a rank of 214,781, that is very high or pretty high in the US. There are so many websites out there so this website is a 214,000 website with the most amount of visits in the US and 435,000 worldwide. So basically we cannot tell exactly how much money they're making but we can know for sure that they are actually making money

Facebook Ads Library

Another way of checking to see if a store is actually profitable or making money is using Facebook ads Library. If we go on facebook.com/ads/library. This is a fantastic tool and it can show you all the ads that the store that you're looking at is running. And that way you can tell whether they're actually making money or if they're not running any ads and they're not making money and they've shut down their operations.

Make sure you go on the top right first and click all.

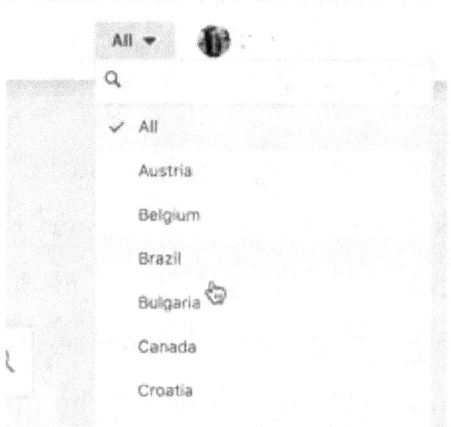

That way you can see all the ads that they're running or else, it's just going to show you the ads for your country. For example if you're in Belgium, it's only going to show you the ads in Belgium so make sure you click on all and then you're going to go and type in the store name.

Q All ads   🏛 Issue, electoral or political

Tufina watches|

Page name contains Tufina watches

Tufina Watches
@tufinauhren · 357.8K likes · Jewellery/watches
@tufina_watches · 60K followers

You can see that this store is really huge. You can see the exact ads that they're running.

Basically these companies can put anything they want on these ads, but you obviously you want to tell the truth, yours doesn't have to be handmade in Germany, you can say designed in Germany, you can say designed in California, made in China. Whatever it is, obviously you're not going to promote that part of it, but you can see the exact ads that they're running which has been making money for them. When you scroll through Facebook, you will always found a ton of amazing product ideas.

Turbo ad Finder

To make this process faster, you can install a Chrome extension called turbo ad finder. What this does is if we turn it on, it actually goes and only shows us ads so most people block the ads but for us dropshippers, it's amazing because it just shows us all of the ads running on Facebook.

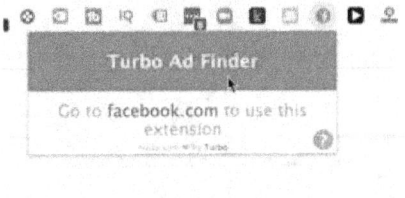

Ecom Hunt (Ecomhunt.com)

Now the next best product research technique that I want to show you is using a tool called Ecom hunt. I don't like promoting a lot of tools but this tool has actually helped me with my own business. I found multiple products with this tool and this one out of all of them out there is the best one that I found, it's only $29 a month.

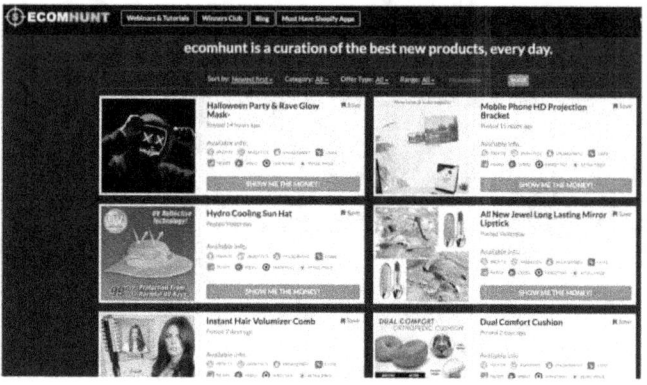

Basically how it works is that it curated list of products every single day and you can go on it and sort the product by orders, and that's what we do here and if we sort by orders it'll basically tell you the highest ordered products. Now this might not be the best if you just sort by orders because these are the products that have the most amount of competition, as well but you shouldn't be afraid of competition anyway because you're following the branded dropshipping approach, then you're creating a brand that is different from everybody else and that's the key to winning against competition.

I'll express it also shows you the CPA from Facebook ads and this is very important as well because this basically tells you how much it's going to cost you in ads for each sale.

Chapter 4

How to Find a Great DropShipping Supplier

This chapter is solely focused on how you can find great suppliers for your dropshipping store

Getting a great supplier is a very important aspect of the whole **business** because if you don't have a good supplier, then your products are going to suck and your store is going to suck and your customers are going to be pissed off, and we don't want that to happen. that's why right now I'm going to show you how to find that the best supplier, the best websites for finding them, and I'm also going to share with you my personal supplier template that I use; it's called the branded dropshipping suppliers template.

This template is something that I came up with based on my earlier experience with selling on Amazon so you know I just took a supplier template that I always use for contacting suppliers on Amazon, and I basically adapted it to Shopify, and you will get this wonderful template without additional costs, you can use that to contact their suppliers.

Key points to remember when contracting suppliers.

1. We're going be using either Alibaba.com or Aliexpress. Now I recommend using Alibaba because most of the products are actually found on Alibaba, some of these products are not available Aliexpress. And another reason you want to get your suppliers on Alibaba is that AliExpress has a

bunch of gimmicky and lower quality products based on my experience.

2. Make sure that the suppliers that you're contacting have millions of dollars in revenue per year, I'm going to show you how to look at that as well.

3. Make sure they there have been in business for at least two years

4. Contact at least three to five suppliers at a minimum because if we only contact one, then we don't have any reference point in terms of prices we don't have any negotiating power because we don't know what the accurate prices are for a particular product and know if we're getting ripped off or if we're getting a fair deal.

The branded dropshipping supplier template

Hello, my name is *Name* and I'm the Lead Purchasing Agent of *Company Name.*

I was looking at your store and I am very interested in creating a long-term business relationship with your company.

Our store specializes in selling *Category of Products* and we are currently selling *# orders* per day and I believe that we can increase our sales by creating a long-term and beneficial working relationship with your company.

Before proceeding, we have a few questions we were hoping you could answer:

1. *Do you offer Blind Dropshipping - or without sending an invoice and any associated marketing materials including in or on the packaging.*

2. *Do you offer Bulk Dropshipping - our store's current selling volume is too large to place orders individually.*

3. *Do you have a MOQ (Minimum Order Quantity) required for any of your products?*

4. *Are you able to send an invoice for the whole bulk dropshipping order at once on Alipay?*

5. *Are you able to apply my company's logo on the products?*

Our company would like to send you an Excel Spreadsheet (CSV) file with each customer's information (full name, email, address, product, etc.) and have you process each order individually by sending each customer their appropriate product.

You would then send our company a full invoice for the whole bulk dropshipping order, which we would gladly pay via Alipay.

Please let us know if you are interested in forming this mutually beneficial, long-term business relationship with us.

Also, please add us on WhatsApp and send us a message there promptly
-> WhatsApp Number

We look forward to doing business with you for many years to come.
Sincerely, Company Name

This is what the branded dropshipping supplier template looks like. You obviously want to change where I put the italic letter so for example, hello "my name is *name*" make sure to change this, or if your supplier sees this then they're going to be like "okay, this person's not serious" and we want to make sure that we look much bigger than we are. You don't want to tell them "hey I'm just a dude, or I'm just a girl trying to start a dropshipping business". You want to make it seem like you're already established. If they start asking you for your website and things like that say, it's under development or like we're redeveloping right now. You also include a company name, just make up a brand name it doesn't have to be the final one that you're going to use. You can always just tell them "this is our new brand name". Trust me, it really doesn't matter, there's a language barrier anyway so here our store specializes in selling category of products put in the category or the niche, and we want to emphasize that we're interested in creating a long-term business relationship with the company.

Chinese suppliers are always interested in creating a long-term business relationship because what that means is, for us they actually want to start dropping because they know that later on we're going to go and start ordering inventories in thousands of units, and that's where they make the real money. That's why this is perfect because it starts off on a good note.

You can also see that the template contains some questions that we're going to ask;

Do you offer blind dropshipping?

Basically there's nothing worse than your customer getting a product that they paid

$50 for on your store, and what happens is that the product that they get has a bunch of Chinese writing on it, Chinese marketing materials, and even worse, it has the invoice that shows that you paid $3 for it. Obviously they're going to be really pissed off. That's what is called blind dropshipping. Some of them don't know what it is, so just explain to them what it is after when you're actually talking to them in chat.

Do you offer bulk dropshipping?

And what that means is we're going to be sending them an excel sheet of our orders. It's very easy to get that from Shopify. You can just do that once every day, or once every two days and you can send them your order sheet and they're will individually fulfil every order and it's going to go straight to your customer. You don't have to ship anything, you don't have to pack anything.

We also asked them for MOQ, if they have a minimum order quantity for any of their products. And very important is, "are you able to apply my company's logo on the products? You always want to try to get your logo on the product, even if it's dropshipping. Sometimes they'll say yes, if you want the logo it's going to be a 50 minimum order quantity or 100 minimum order quantity and that's because that's just the way that their printing system works. And so in that case, try to negotiate down. just say 'hey you know we're just doing a test and so that's why we can't order the MOQ right now, but if you can print the logo on the product and you can dropship it, then we're going to order thousands of units later. Through that way, they're will be more willing to do it.

Also we explained how we're going to do it. So our company's going to send you an Excel spreadsheet file with each customer's information so full name, e-mail address, and product and having processes each order individually. And then basically they would send us an invoice and we pay via PayPal, or wire transfer. I recommend PayPal but if you have a trusted supplier you've already have established a good relationship with, wire transfer is totally fine. And then at the bottom, you put in your WhatsApp number. I highly recommend communicating with your supplier via WhatsApp because the Aliexpress and Alibaba messaging platforms are extremely clunky, and it's just going to take days to negotiate a proper price where the same negotiations could have taken place via WhatsApp and it would have taken way less time. And at the bottom make sure to put in your company name.

Now I'm going to show you how to find trusted suppliers on Aliexpress and Alibaba. If we go on Aliexpress and let's say you want to dropship flexible selfie stick for instance, just type in flexible selfie stick and hit enter

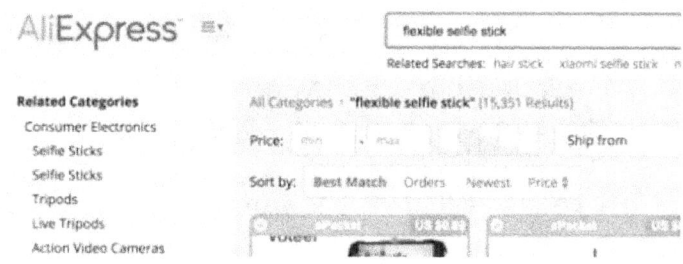

Note that the page will display several results and you may see some products that are looks good but are quite expensive, most likely such a products is from a trader, someone who's in China and who's just sitting on their computer cutting deals between factories and people who are trying to dropship like us, and so they're pocketing the cash. You want to avoid that. You can search the products by orders or by best match.

If you do find a supplier here and you think that they're good, just click on them and it will take you to the product page. Now at this point, we don't want to do what every other person out there is doing; which is simply to use Oberlo and copy and paste these products on their store. We want to contact them and try to get our logo on this product and that's what branded dropshipping is about. Trust me, there's not going to be a long-term successful store that's just going to dropship without a logo, it can be a great product but only if it's backed by a solid brand.

Next click on contact now and this is where you're going to go and copy paste the template

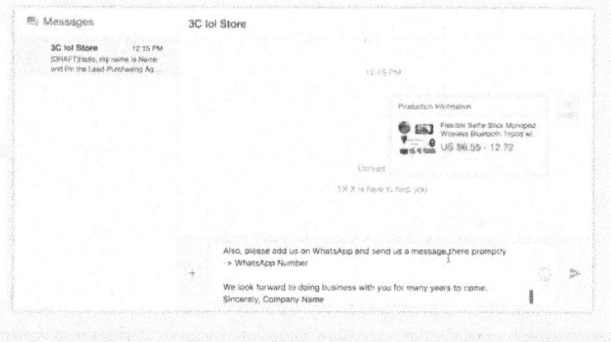

Make sure that you add your name and remove the title of the template, put in your WhatsApp number too.

If you observe closely, you will something called epacket on some of the listed products, epacket is the trade agreement between China and US; epacket is a slightly faster method of shipping from China. Instead of it taking like 4weeks to get products to the customer, it might take 2-3 weeks. Now with branded dropshipping, we can always try to ask them for DHL shipping, that way they'll ship via DHL it will be more expensive but its way faster. it'll take like three to five days from China and then eventually we move on over to branding the private labeling on our store and that is the key, that is how you build a multi-million dollar store that will set you up for life.

Now if we head to Alibaba, the process is basically the same, however I found a lot of amazing products there and just much better suppliers overall, and honestly you can find such amazing suppliers here. When searching for products you have to dig sometimes the products are on one but not the other.

Alibaba is better because you have a much higher chance of actually contacting the factory instead of just the trader who's making money off of you on AliExpress.

Follow the same process of contacting the supplier, and for quantity, even though we're dropshipping put in 1000 units, if you put in 1000 units, trust me a supplier who sees a $1000 dollar or 1000 quantity message will always want to reply faster than something that has only one quantity. Just copy and paste the template again without the title, and make sure to change the name and put your company or brand name at the appropriate places and send your inquiry.

Chapter 5

Setting Up Your Shopify Store

Let's get into actually setting up our store and the actual design of it as well, basically putting it all together so that it looks great for our customers. I assume by now that you've already sign up for your Shopify free trial, if not then just go to Shopify.com to go and set up your free trial. It's going to bring you to a page that's similar to this and you're going to want to put an email address a password and your store name.

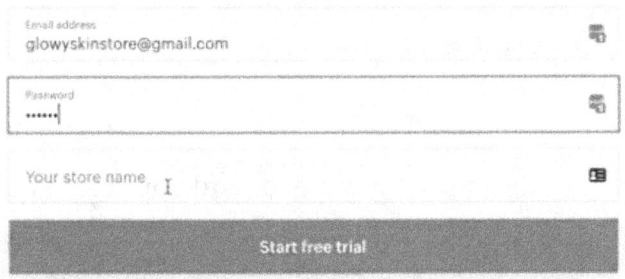

If you already know what your product is, as well as what your brand name is, then I recommend don't use your personal email address. You can go and temporarily set up a Gmail under your store name. Let's say that our store name is going to be glowy skin you can put glowy skin store, or glowy skin official, or glowy skin support at gmail.com. This is only temporary because we want to have our support email look more legitimate and I'm going to explain how to get an actual domain name email later on. If your actual store name isn't available, then just put in Co at the end. And also as you're doing this, I highly recommend you go and check if you can get the domain name for your store.

If you don't buy a domain then, store is not going to be professional and your store link will be something like glowyskin.Shopify.com, hit start free trial get to this part right here and it's going to say success your store is ready to go and so now it's going to say tell us a little bit about yourself

I'm going to walk you through step- by -step what put in here. If you are you already selling, you can just put I'm selling just not online or you can put I am not selling products yet. The next question is, do you have something to sell? Say yes I have a product I'll be ready to launch soon. For current revenue you can put like up to $5000, or I'm just getting started. It doesn't really matter. If you put down higher numbers here, then you're going to get a call from a Shopify specialist and they're basically try to sell you on their enterprise plan so that's why it's better to just put like $5000 or zero and then click next. On the next page you want to add an address so you can get paid.

Add an address so you can get paid

This will be used as your default business address

First name

Last name

Address

Apartment, suite, etc. (optional)

City: Toronto

ZIP/Postal code

Country/Region: Canada

Province: Ontario

Phone number

Business or personal website (optional): example.com

This is your default business address so just put in the address either of your house where you live or of your registered business if you already have an LLC or a corporation then just put the address of that business. If you don't have that, you don't necessarily need that to start. However, I recommend getting that set up in your home country. it will save you a lot of money in taxes and a lot of headache so just go ahead and put your first name last name in your address and then put your phone number and then your domain if you already have a domain, if not ,then you can just leave it blank because we're going to be covering buying a domain in a later section in this book and then click enter my store.

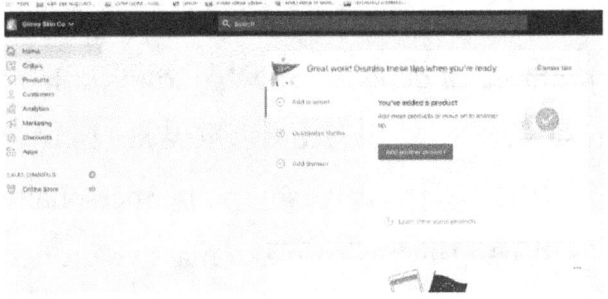

Now we're in our new Shopify store and this is the dashboard. This is what it will look like. Once you start making sales you'll see that there's going to be a lot of new things that pop up, like how much money you're making and you can do a breakdown of every single day, every single month and you can see things like your conversion rate and all that kind of stuff. For now it's pretty basic we don't have a lot of stuff here and it's we need to add a product, add a theme, and a domain.

So the first thing we're going to do is to add a theme. Now, there are free themes and paid themes. Both free and paid themes are okay, you don't need a paid theme to make profit, it all depends on what kinds of look you want for your store. There are tons of free themes you can use, and I've personally used free themes to make massive profits. But if you really want to go away from the generic Shopify look then I recommend getting a paid theme they're not even that expensive.

How to select themes for your store

Click on online store and then themes and then scroll down and click on Shopify theme store and then visit theme store

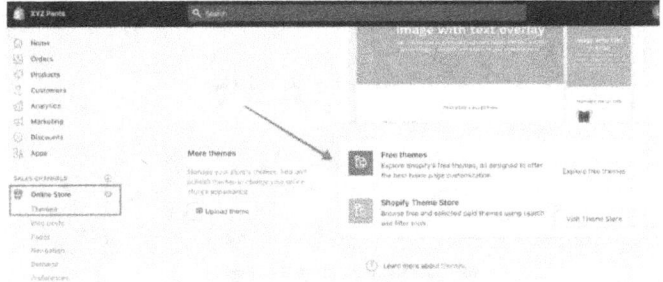

So here is where you can get all the themes that you need. You can just play around with things, you can go to collections and check the different styles of themes available.

Choose your preferred theme it's going to install the theme on your store so now it's going to say are you sure you want to publish debut click publish.

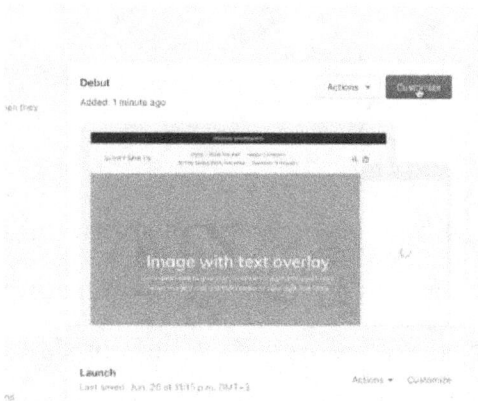

So now the theme is live on our store and if we go and we click customize so now we're in our theme and as you can see it just says the store name glowy skin Co

The next thing we want to do is to add your store logo, if you don't know how to create one, you can simply head to canvas to create a simple logo to use for your store. Make sure your logo really fits into your product niche. If you don't like to do this yourself you can head to Fiverr or Upwork and get some really good graphics designers to help you get this done. If you are using Canvas, always download your logo as a PNG file with a transparent background.

The next part is going to involve uploading some pictures to our website. We need really good pictures for our brand store. It is really important with branded dropshipping if you want to succeed to present your product in the best possible light. And to do that, we have to make sure that we have some professional quality pictures.

How do you go about this? You're going to need to get one sample of your product to your house so you can see them and take pictures of them, or so you can send them out to a photographer if needed. How this works is when you're going to be talking to your supplier on WhatsApp, just ask for a sample and they're going to charge you typically more than what one unit would usually cost, but that's because it's just more expensive for them to produce a sample with your logo. And you want to make sure that they produce the sample with your logo, and then they're going to send it off to your house. You have to wait until that comes and once it arrives, you can go and either take pictures of it yourself, you want a few pictures on a white background, and then also you want to get some lifestyle pictures as well. If you have a nice enough camera or you can even try using your iPhone. iPhone camera is good enough, you can go and just take your pictures of your product being used so you want pictures of every angle on a white background and then you want pictures with your product being used so outside or in the environment where your product is usually being used.

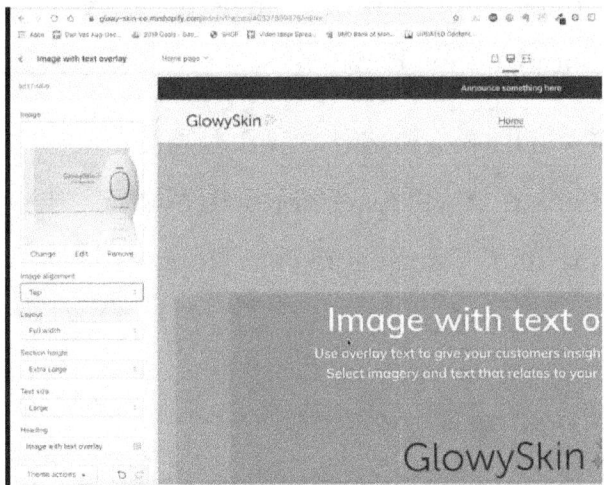

If you have a competitor for your product, I recommend looking your competition just to get ideas. We don't want to copy our competition, I don't want you to take advantage of people and not actually sell and build something of value for our world right. you're going to use competitors just as inspiration, just to see what kind of text headlines they're using because obviously it's working don't reinvent the wheel there's no need to just come at it from a different angle, from your own angle improve on it but just don't copy.

I will leave a resource at the end of the book that will teach you step by step method of setting up your store.

Creating Store Pages

Since Shopify and your prospective customers doesn't have any idea of what your store is all about, you need to create ages that will help you to provide more information about your store to the prospective customers.

I recommend that you create the following pages for your shopify dropshipping store

1. About Us

2. Contact Us

3. Shipping & Returns

4. Order Status

5. Terms of Service

6. Privacy Policy

To create a new page, simply click on the "pages" tab under online store in the dashboard, then click "Add page"

When the next screen appears, put in the tile of the page and then write in the content for that page.

Once you are done imputing your content, click on save and repeat this procedure for all your order pages and then move navigation settings

Setting up you store Navigation

After creating the pages of your store, then you need to visualize how you want your customers to navigate your Shopify store. Most stores want prospective customers to browse their product collections and about us page before moving to any other part of the website, therefore it is common to have these elements placed at the top of the store's homepage.

Other pages such as Privacy Policy and Terms of Service are usually placed at the footer section of the website.

Once you've determined the pages you want at the top menu or footer section of your website, then follow the steps below to create your store's navigation

Select navigation from the left hand corner of your screen

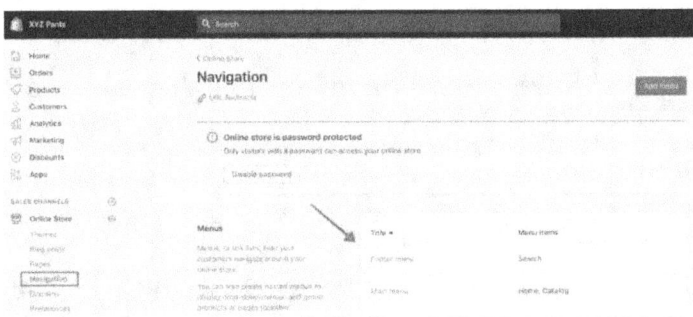

Next choose the header or footer menu

Then click on "Add menu Item".

Assign a name to this item, then go to the "link" option to choose it from a list of pages, products and collections you've already created. Repeat the steps until your header and footer menu gets populated.

Setting up Shopify payments

Since you are running your business online, you want to make different payment options available to shoppers so that they can checkout from your store with whichever payment option they are most comfortable with.

The major method of payment for online transactions is credits cards and PayPal. Shopify has an excellent payment feature which you can use to receive your money directly via the platform.

To see the available payment methods in your country, go to "Settings" then choose "payment providers"

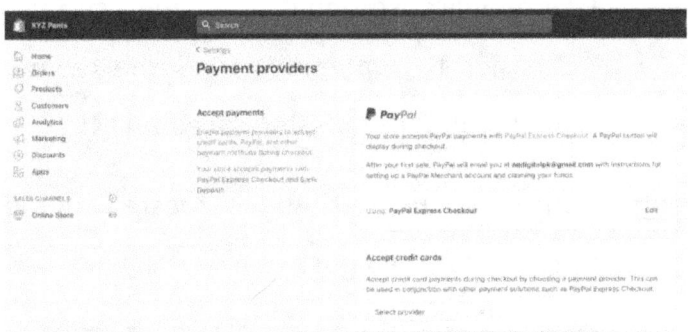

There are different options available to you through which you can get your payment. Activate the ones you that is suitable for you and provide additional information such as your bank account number to make sure that the money gets to the right place

Choosing a Domain for your Shopify Dropping store#

In order to present yourself as a serious business, you need to get a domain name for your Shopify store. It is great for our branded dropshipping approach and also far easier to remember than the default nameofyourstore.myshopify.com URL

Your domain settings is located under Online Store category

When you get to the domain page, you will are given the options to either purchase a new domain, connect your existing domain

or transfer your domain to Shopify. The first option allows you to purchase a domain directly through Shopify. This cost $14 per year. If you have an existing domain you've previously purchased, all you need do is to connect it to Shopify. You can always buy your domains from GoDaddy and Namecheap. A premium .com domain will cost you just $ on these sites.

Once you've set up your website and is fully ready to run, you can sign up for a paid Shopify plan.

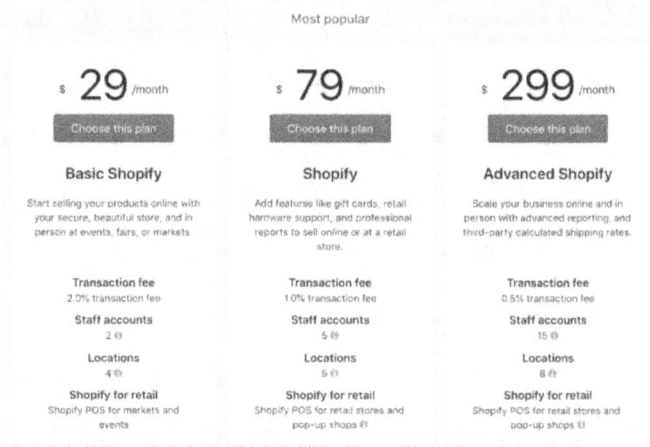

Even though the free trial gives you access to the full features of Shopify, the truth is that you can't make any sales until you subscribed to a monthly plan.

Chapter 6

The Absolute Best Apps to Use for Your Store

Let's talk about the apps we should install on our store. The very best apps to use in 2020, 2021 and beyond.

The App Store in Shopify has grown and continues to grow a lot so that's why there's always new apps coming out that do things better. There are lots of free as well as paid apps in the store, but I always recommend the pay ones because they'll make you way more profit than the free apps, don't worry about their costs because they will pay off themselves.

To start installing your apps, just go to visit Shopify App Store

My Recommended Apps

1. Order Lookup app

We're going to start with the order lookup app. The app allows us to install an order look-up on to our store. This is great because if we're having our supplier ship the order or if we're doing fulfilment centers, then your customer can just get a tracking number and go to your website and then they can go at the top and there's going to be like an order lookup number.

Just search for the app and install, and after installing click verify my store and their team is going to go and verify your store.

2. Help Center

Help center is basically a FAQ app. It allows us to have a nice looking frequently ask questions section on our page. To Get FAQs for your page, you can simply visit your competitor's website and just structure your questions like theirs.

3. Loox Reviews

Another great app is Loox eviews. And this one allows us to have picture reviews on our page. And actually this lets you write your own reviews at the very beginning. And that's what I usually do because at the beginning, you don't have any social proof, (your customers that are posting reviews on your product) and so that's why it's difficult to actually start selling at the beginning. But this lets you actually post your own reviews you can go and download an excel sheet and you can fill in some reviews maybe from your previous customers or from friends and family you can just go put in some names. It is going to cost $10 a month after the 14 day free trial.

4. SMS Bump

The next app we want to install is called SMS bump. This is an amazing app that lets you send out automatic text to potential customers. If someone goes on your sales page and they don't buy, you or your staff can just go and send them a text saying, hey you know come back to the store here's a 20% off coupon! And that's worked insanely for me I've had like a 9000% return on investment just using this app, so super super recommend. This app is really great I recommend you to install this as you will be able to get so many more sales and make so much more profit on autopilot just with this app.

5. klaviyo

The next app we're going to install is called klaviyo. This is the email marketing app that I like to use. Usually these are free to install and then as soon as you actually start doing volume with them then they're actually going to cost money. So at that moment you're actually going to start making sales hopefully so by that time you're not just going to be charged for apps.

6. Recart

Recart is a great app. basically it allow you to go and set up sequences that you send to your customers in their Facebook messages. These are known to have way higher open rates which means people look at them way more than just emails. So if you're hitting them from Facebook

Messenger, from email, and from SMS, it's huge. You're going to make so much more money doing this, so I recommend you install recart.

7. Bold Multi Currency

This is an Automatic currency converter. Basically if someone comes from Canada your price willbe in Canadian dollars, a visitor from United States gets to see your price in US dollars, someone comes from Europe it's in Euros. I also recommend installing this one if you're going to be selling internationally.

8. Easy Location

This is an automatic geoip redirect app. So basically this redirects the user to the appropriate store language on your page. so for example this would be great if let's say I'm selling in France, Spain and USA if someone comes from France and I have a

French version of my store it will redirect them to the fr page of my store so it's really a great app.

9. Oberlo

If you want to actually go and use the old way of copying and pasting products from Aliexpress you would need Oberlo. Although this is not branded dropshipping you're basically just copying and pasting and like I said this method doesn't really worked out well, but if you want to do it, then you can use the oberlo app.

How to use Oberlo

If you prefer to go the Oberlo way even though I don't so much recommend, it, this is the step you need to take

Click on the products tab in the left corner of your Shopify dashboard

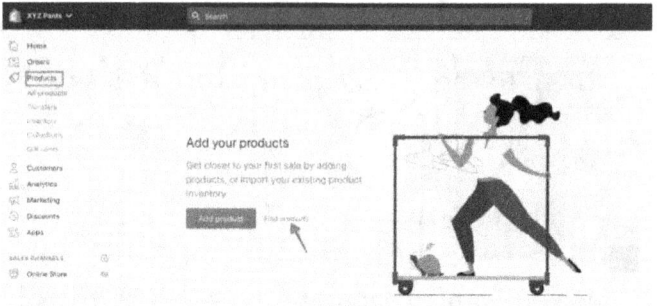

Next click on "Find products" then in the next window click "find products now"

You will get prompted that you are about to install Oberlo, click on install app in the down right corner to continue

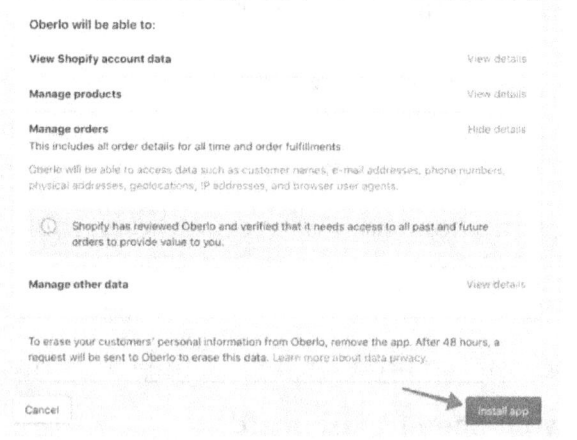

After installing the app, Oberlo's interface will be made available to you and from here you can search for products and suppliers. Just enter some product name into the search bar and click the search button to see a list of results.

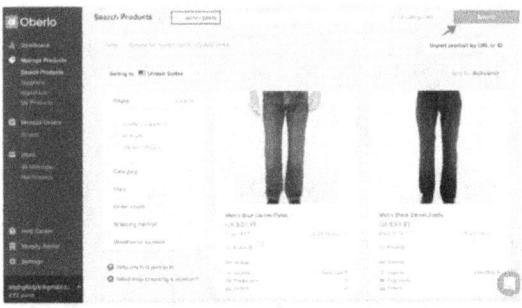

Just browse through the listed products and choose the items you preferred. If you want to check the product page, click on "Select Products". On the products page you will be able to review the pricing and shipping details, then click on Add product. The selected items will be added to your Shopify store.

Chapter 7

Marketing Your Dropshipping Business

It will be practically impossible for you to sell your products if no one knows about them or if your brand is very unpopular. How can a total stranger trust your product, your brand? This is where the magic of marketing comes in, if properly done, it will make total strangers have total trust in you to hand over their money to you happily.

The field of marketing is quite subjective and there are millions of strategies that can be employed to strategically position your brand while improving your brand awareness and generating massive sales in the process. If your strategy is well-laid out, it can even help you ward off stiff competitions.

Email Marketing

If you overlook email marketing that's a huge mistake because email marketing is a huge part of becoming profitable with your Shopify store. There's two things in a regular Shopify store; that's the front end and the back end this is applicable to any business. The difference between the front end and the back end is that the front end is where people go to on our store, they see our ad and they buy from our actual sales page, that's called a front end sale.

But most of the money will actually be made on your back end. On your front end, you can never rely on just running ads and basically just having to get new customers to your store and purchase your product, it's always better to sell again to the same customer than it is to have to acquire a new customer. That's just basic rules of marketing. That's why we have to develop our backend, and setting up our email marketing is a part of that, as well as SMS and then Facebook Messenger.

Building a good email list involves having highly targeted and constantly engaged recipients. If you have a good email list, it might just be your most important marketing asset! An email list allows you to have direct access to your customers, you don't have to spend extra money to acquire customers, and you don't have to spend money to get your emails delivered to their inboxes. And most important, you avoid having to compete with other sellers if you have a great email list. Email marketing remains one of the most effective direct ways to engage with your customers.

It is not so difficult to build an email list, you only need to get visitors to your store drop their emails to you and then send out emails to them periodically through a tool like Klaviyo which I recommend you installed earlier.

Social Media for Your Dropshipping Business

The Social media remains one of the most effective ways of advertising, promoting, and acquiring customers, in order to generate thousands and millions of dollars in profits. Facebook for instance has over 2.45 billion monthly active users from all walks of life.

Facebook and Instagram are huge channels today. People are on Facebook all the time so you're going to want to target people on Facebook. And the targeting is so intense that you can get right in front of the person that would be perfect for your product. So one example like that is, let's say, that you sell gymnastics equipment to kids, maybe to girls, in particular. You could actually target mothers that make over $50,000 a year that have daughters that are in gymnastics. How targeted is that? If these mothers see these ads, they can afford it, right? They're making enough money to afford it. They have daughters in gymnastics. It just only makes sense. They're going to like your product and they're going to understand your brand, and they're going to eventually buy from you. So make sure you take advantage of Facebook and Instagram ads. Those two channels are big breadwinners for ecommerce stores today.

Instagram influencers

Influencers are amazing, businesses have been built to the billions of dollars just on influencers. Right now, we live in the influencer age and that's why I'm going to tell you how to properly use influencers and find the right ones to grow your Shopify store. This is fantastic if you only have about 200 or 300 dollars as a starting budget, because if you have more money than that, I would say just go directly into Facebook Ads. A mix of influencers and ads is always best, but if you have like only 200-300 dollars, then that might not be enough for proper Facebook Ads for the best results

There are a lot of influencers out there, the best ones that I found have between 10,000 to 100,000 followers, and there's another group of them that have from 100,000 – 250,000 followers. Now we always want to try to send them a free product to have them make a video with our product, just a quick little video or have them post the product on their page. What I like to do is I like to send them a DM, and you're going to have to DM them probably once every single day. What you do is you just send them a DM and then you unsend it if they didn't see it, and then you send it again. You can actually unsend DMs on Instagram.

And what I like to do is, I always like to put emoji's, so you just put emoji's at the top of your message and that really gets their attention. What you do is you offer a product for free; and you message them from the Instagram page of your store. And of course by now, you would have uploaded some pictures of your actual product on your store, and you would have started engaging with some people and you would have started liking some associated pages, if you're just messaging from a new account with one or two followers, no one's going to answer that.

So what we always want to do is we want to try to send them a free product, and if you don't have a way to send them a product with fast 2-3 days shipping, then what you can do is you can just go to Amazon and you can buy a product and send it directly to them from Amazon, even though it's not your brand, you can have it sent to them even though this isn't really ethical, and this only works if you don't have a logo already on your product. It is an option and I mean it's pretty funny but it does work, or if you can have a way to have your product sent out very fast from your supplier as a sample with the logo on it, then always do that because then you'll have a logo and what you can do is you can tell them "hey just free product in in exchange for a shout-out on your page" and you will also want to check to make sure that not only do they have followers but also that are legitimate people that their follower base is actually active, they're interested in what they're posting and they're not fake. If you find a really good page, or a really good influencer with a 100,000 or 50,000 followers, then you can offer to pay them. Always ask them first what their fee is, and you can always negotiate it down so you can pay $50, $100, $200 for a shout. I've paid $20 before and made back like $30,000, so it really depends, sometimes you pay and you get nothing, sometimes you pay and you hit a jackpot.

But if you don't want to pay any money, micro influencers are amazing and these are basically people on Instagram, they're not celebrities. Most of their followers are just their friends and these people have between 1,000 and 10,000 followers. I'm sure you know people like that. And they're not celebrities at all, they're just normal people that like to hang out on Instagram, and so you just DM them, you say "hey free product" and then they'll go and they'll post it and their friends will see it and they'll also maybe send you DM asking you for a free product. That way, your product spreads with word-of-mouth marketing and that's always more powerful than paid marketing.

Killer ecommerce marketing strategy tips.

Ecommerce marketing can be super complicated. There's just so many different things that you can do. And so in this section, I'm going to break down 8 tips that we recommend you really focus on first. If you dial these in, you're going to be successful online.

Tip number 1

Spend a tremendous amount of time optimizing your product pages with regards to SEO and design. So what I mean by that is SEO would be a good product title, OK? Don't just call it something that only you would know. Call it something within the title that people are actually searching online. So do some keyword research, figure out what people are searching for and make that part of your product title. Also, include that in the description of the product. Write a good description. Remember, this is your 24/7 salesperson. Your product page never calls in sick. It works through the weekends and the holidays.

Every time somebody visits your product page, they want your perfect sales pitch, so put some time into that.

Also, product photography, hugely important. Make sure that photography is really, really clean, smooth, and a nice design, and professional. And also, if you can do a product video, this is massively valuable. Make sure you invest in doing some product videos to explain your products in more details. Final tips here, make sure you have trust badges on the page.

Make sure it says things like you have fast shipping, free shipping, all of that, if you have that.

And also, get reviews of your products. You want to have reviews on your product pages. Studies show if you have reviews on your product pages that can increase your conversion rate significantly, up to 400%.

So make sure that you get product reviews on your page.

Tip number 2

Run Google Shopping ads. Google Shopping is very, very popular. People go to Google. They'll search something like pink shoes, they'll click the shopping tab, and those are all ads. So if you want to be in that shopping tab, which we highly recommend, you're going to want to make sure that you are running Google Shopping ads. So invest in running product ads. And then here's a tip, optimize your product ads based on results. So if you have ecommerce tracking set up, you can see the revenue generated from each product. You can really see your ROI, per product, on your product ads. What you want to do is as time goes by, turn off the ads that aren't doing as well, the products that aren't doing as well, and increase the budget on the products that are doing well. This is going to really increase your return on investment over time.

Tip number 3
Run Dynamic Retargeting Campaigns

Run dynamic retargeting campaigns off of your Google Shopping ads and your website visitors so that people that go to your website and they browse maybe two, three products. As they're surfing the internet after that on the Google Display Network which has thousands of websites online, they're going to see banner ads for your brand actually showing the specific products that they looked at. So it's very relevant. This stays top of mind and it kind of just wears them down until they are ready to buy those products. They click it, and they purchase on your website. Also, you can run retargeting on Facebook and Instagram as well. So if somebody comes to your site, they look around and they don't do anything, that night when they're on Facebook kind of looking through their feed, all of a sudden they'll see an ad for your brand. This is bringing you back to the top of their mind. They're like, "hey, I didn't have time earlier to put my credit card in there because I was getting interrupted, but hey, I do right now on this commercial that's on TV, so I'm going to buy right now. So by doing retargeting in a dynamic way, you're going to bring a lot more sales back to your business.

Tip number 4

Invest in Your Social Media Organically

Whether you need to do this yourself or hire somebody or hire another company, you need to make sure you have an organic presence on social media. What that means is you're posting content, you're engaging on social media. So not paid ads, but just being involved, being a part of social media today. By doing this, this is going to be building your brand following organically. So eventually you have 10,000 followers, 100,000 followers. The more followers you have as you're posting content, building this awareness, you're only going to get more sales.

Tip number 5

Automate Your Email Marketing

Tip number five is to automate your email marketing. Email marketing is hugely important. A lot of ecommerce stores fall short because they spend a lot of money to get that customer to make that first purchase, but they don't re-market to those people via email marketing and other channels to get them to come back and make future purchases. If you could just get each of your customers to make one more purchase than they normally do, think about what that does to your revenue. So with email marketing, it allows us an automated way to make that happen. If you're creative with your email marketing and you automate it, this is going to scale your business so that you can increase your sales overall and increase your return on investment on your marketing dollars.

Tip number 6
Invest in SMS marketing

SMS marketing is text message marketing. The reason why that's important is because only about 20% of people will typically open up your emails, sometimes even less. And they also won't open it up in real time. There's a lag there, right? But with text messages, it's almost 100% of people open the text message. And most of them are within a five-minute window. So that can be really powerful on slow sales days, on end of the month, times when you need to clear out old inventory, stuff like that. So build a VIP text message marketing campaign. And one way to do this is put a banner on your site that says, hey, for VIP deals, text something like hot deals to 39970 to opt in and get an immediate 20% coupon right now. By doing that, it gets people to opt in to get that coupon, but now they're in that list for future VIP deals that you can tap into when you need to.

Tip number 7
Use a CRM

Tip number 7 is to use a CRM. So many ecommerce stores don't really have a CRM. They're actually using the backend of their cart to look at customer data and using that as a CRM. That's not effective. You want to integrate your cart with an actual CRM so that you can populate all of your customer data and even add additional data in there, as you get to know your customer. And so if you hire a salesperson or if you're the salesperson, working through the CRM and actually making proactive calls to your customers can be life-changing for your business. If you just reach out and say, hey, how was it? Did you get your package in time? Is everything going OK for you? What else are you interested in? Can I keep an eye out for other deals that come up and let you know? Do you have any kids? When are their birthdays? What are they interested in? If you get to know the customer, you can save this information in your CRM. Your salesperson can just continually follow up with these people. And I'm telling you, you'll see four or five times more sales per customer than you would otherwise. So it's a huge investment, but a great return to look at a salesperson in CRM and connecting those into your process within your ecommerce business.

Tip number 8

Create a Customer Care Package

Last tip is to create a customer care package that you send with all of your product purchases to the customer. So don't just send them a bag with a logo on it. Send them a nice package that has a handwritten note. It has a coupon in it for a future purchase. It maybe has a referral card in there they can give to a friend. This is going to be a nice experience for the customer, and it's really going to give them a good sense of feeling towards your brand, and probably get them to come back and purchase with you again.

But one really hot tip here is if you're selling on other channels, such as Amazon or something like that, when you send those products with a care package, the coupon and whatnot should recommend they come back to your branded website to make future purchases. This is going to increase your profitability and get your brand going on your own website, which is what you want to do. So take advantage of these care packages. Design something real nice so when they receive your product, you stand out in the crowd from other businesses you may be competing against.

Ecommerce is super intense. We could go for days with different tips, but these 8 tips I feel like are really the ones that are the most important. So focus on these tips

Chapter 8

How to Handle Refunds, Returns & Replacements for Dropshipped Products

Dropshipping is an online business, therefore it is inevitable that you will have to deal with refunds, returns and replacements. Initially, this may seem dispiriting, however it's just part and parcel of running an online store. You cannot achieve a 100% customer satisfaction no matter how hard you try. There are three situations that may make your customers return and demand a refund. These are well elucidated below.

Products is faulty

The first situation that may warrant a customer to demand refund is when your drop shipper send a faulty product to them. So how do you handle such a situation?

Is it outside of product guarantee? If yes then explain and offer to replace it if they return it to you (if you need to). What I would do here is, if it's outside of that guarantee that you offer, then go back to them by email or on Facebook Messenger, however they've contacted you and just explain that it's out that guarantee and unfortunately because of that, then we're no longer offering a refund. In most cases, people will be fine with that people expect that, noting that not everything comes with a lifetime guarantee. So you might not hear from them again.

However, you might get that one person that won't take no for an answer, they'll keep demanding a refund and maybe even threaten to open a PayPal dispute. When that happens, it's completely up to you guys how you play it. For me personally, if it's not a large value order, then I'll just back to them and say, look out of goodwill then we will offer to refund it but you must send it back to us and it must be in the original condition.

Request evidence photo or video: We live in a day and age where pretty much everyone should be able to get hold of a photo of the product or a video of it, just ask them to send it to you showing the product is indeed faulty. And then if it is faulty, you can either let them keep it or ask them to return it to you and then you can give them the choice you can say we can offer you a full refund or we can send you a new one.

If they send the picture or video and you discovered that it is not faulty, try to

explain how to work it or how it should work.

If you can find a way of explaining by email or messenger how to work it and fix the problem before you get to the stage of asking them to send it back or offer a refund.

The last point is ultimately, if the customers is unhappy, offer to refund or send a new one so what this means is then every now and again it will happen you'll get a funny customer that no matter what you do just doesn't seem to make them happy so in that case you want to get rid of them as quickly as possible whilst trying to keep them as happy as possible, especially being a new business where no one's heard of you. One bad review can just completely sabotage your business. So just try and do whatever you can to keep them happy. And if you need to take a loss on that particular order, then trust me it's worth it.

Products Is Okay But Like To Return

Moving on to the next situation, we've got products is okay but like to return it. So every now and again, you'll get someone who receives their product and for whatever reason they just don't want it anymore, so again is it outside of that product guarantee? If it is, then you can play it two ways; you can play hardball and just explain and say, "Look, I'm sorry, it's outside the guarantee, there's nothing we can do". Or you can ask if it is in its original condition. Again, ask them for a photo and if it is, then ask them to return it and make a full refund.

If it's not outside of the guarantee then just simply ask them to return it and once you've received it, then just refund them in full. It is up to you if customer has to pay for the shipping. Obviously you don't want it to be out of your pocket because it's not your fault, it's the customer who's changed their mind. But then at the same time, you want to keep the customer happy. So explain that because it's them that changed their mind, that they're liable for shipping. But ultimately this should be clearly stated in your terms and condition. So if there is any throw back from it, then you can always pull that card. However from personal experience, the best thing you can always do is keep the customer happy. Ultimately if the customer is unhappy, offer to refund or send a new one. Because someone can just completely sabotage your business, they can go on all your social media pages leave bad reviews on your website. So as a last resort, just do whatever you can to keep it to get rid of the customer.

The Product Has Not Arrived

The final situation that may make a customer demand refund is if the product has not arrived.

As we are dropshipping, there is a lot that can go wrong between the product being shipped from China and arriving at the customer's home. This is probably one of the most popular situations you'll have to deal with. So if it's within your quoted delivery times, then politely ask the customer to wait. You can go back to them and say, "look I apologize it's taking so long." However make sure you clearly states the delivery time on the product page and then you can send them the tracking code.

If it is outside the quoted delivery time, it's taking a bit longer than what you actually quoted, then just make sure you apologize to the customer. Give a reason, people don't usually accept something unless you explain why, so make sure you give a valid reason. You can either say something along the lines of "it got lost" and then offer to send them a new order.

At some point you'll get a customer that comes on to you and says, "look, I've had enough of this, I'm not waiting anymore give me my money back." What I would do in that situation there if the order has been dispatched and it's within the quoted delivery time, then I would usually go back to them and say, "look unfortunately it's been dispatched, here's the tracking code so you can clearly see that it's still within our quote of delivery times which you accepted so please wait until the order has arrived, and if you would still like a refund then please return it and we'll be more than happy to do so." Now that will work for the majority of the time, however there will still be a small percentage of people that will come back to you and say, "no it's still not good enough, I want my money back." And if it gets to that point, then ultimately you want to keep your customer happy and unfortunately you have to take the hit and just give them the money back.

Where does the Customer send the Return Item?

This is probably the most popular part of dealing with returns. And for me I consider three major options as your best solution. The first one being a virtual office, that's the option I use. The advantage of a virtual office is that it looks professional, it protects your home address, no one can know what your home address is, you have the option to either go or collect them yourself or they'll forward it to your home address.

The second option is your home. However, it looks unprofessional if they're sending it to a street address plus they get your home address which probably isn't a good idea, but it is free, it doesn't cost you any money, so if you are on a very tight budget then it's always an option. to be honest when I first started, I use my home address for about 3-4 weeks, but then when I started selling more my returns increased, that's when I then migrated to a virtual office.

And then third option then in case you're not aware of this but Walmart offer a P.O box service, and you've probably seen it before where you write a company name and then just a PA box number. What happens is when someone post it to a P.O box, Walmart will sort it and they'll deliver it to your local post office and then you can go and collect it from that post office. So again, it looks professional because it's like a proper address, it protects your personal address and is not so expensive.

What to Do When Dropshipping Products Are Out Of Stock

If a customer has placed an order on your store and the product is out of stock, all you need do is to put the product on backorder in your supplier's inventory and communicate to your customer that you won't be able to fulfil the order immediately. Give them the choice of waiting till you have the product in stock again or for a full refund. The important thing is to communicate with your customers clearly on whether you will have product in stock again anytime soon. If you aren't so sure, take a calculated guess and let them know the time. Honesty and communication with your customer is the best approach in this situation.

Customer Support for your Dropshipping Business

Having a good customer support system in place can determine how successful your dropshipping business will be. Due to how competitive the dropshipping industry is, having a good customer support system can really do wonders for your brand.

Here are the most commonly used and popular types of customer support system in the ecommerce industry:

Phone Support: Having a phone customer support system in place is one of the fastest and most effective ways of connecting directly with the customer. Not only is it easier to resolve difficult situations, but it is also the fastest way to get feedback from your customer. Google provides tools like Google Voice which allows you set up a free number that routes calls to any number specified by you. Similar alternatives include the OpenPhone (which is precisely made for ecommerce businesses) and Hushed.

Email Support: Although the telephone is a common method of customer support, email is more likely to be your primary method of providing support. It is recommended you set up domain emails for your store (example: hello@yourstore.com). Not only is this professional but this also establishes your brand as a legitimate entity in the mind of your customers. Gorgias is an excellent email support software on Shopify ecommerce platform.

Social Media Support: Customers most times go to the social media pages of brands sometimes even before contacting the brand itself. This is due to the fact that social media is a public forum, and more often than not customers will already get the answers to their questions on the brand's social media page. A good customer support representative on social media will definitely engage with the audience even if the feedback is not so desirable. This can help establish good faith between a customer and the brand.

Live Chat Support: Many brands are integrating live chats on their websites as part of their customer service and support systems. This method is becoming increasingly popular because it is as quick as a phone call, yet less intimidating then posting questions on a public forum. If you have no fund to invest in this yet, you can just use social media such as Facebook Messenger, or the direct message services on platforms such as Instagram and Twitter. Live chat customer support may not be the best option for you if your business is still limited to one person, but it is worth exploring when you have scaled up. Check out Gorgias as well to launch live chat on your Shopify store.

Final Tips for Long term Success

Congratulations you were able to get to the end of this book. I'm super happy that you did because you're part of the few people who are really committed to changing their life, people who are committed to building an online business in today's time of opportunity and abundant, that's why I'm so happy that you're here and you're not part of all those other people who are just trying to basically do things the easy way. Because there's no easy way to do things, it's pretty simple everything that you've read in this book is definitely not easy because we're building a real business, this is not some kind of a gimmick, it's not some kind of trick and you've seen that it is really powerful what it can do in your life.

Now you know everything you need to start a successful branded dropshipping store, and I'm so happy that you the information you needed to kickstart your dropshipping joiurney in this book. Now I want to end this book with some very important tips for Shopify success because I see so many people trying to start this business so many who will try to get into e-commerce and they fail and the biggest reasons why people fail at it all comes down to a few reasons to be honest.

Tip number 1

The biggest tip for you to not fail, to actually succeed is to take action. If you have been taking action as you were reading this book, that's amazing, you're part of the few who are serious about changing their life. If not, then just go ahead and read again and then follow step by step as you're actually taking action because reading and absorbing knowledge is one thing, but putting it into practice is completely different, because that's what will actually make you successful and what will make you thousands and hundreds of thousands of dollars .

Tip number 2

Once you get started with Shopify don't give up. You will not make your first sale in the first 14 days free trial. The free trial honestly is just there for you to just be able to get used to the Shopify layout, to the system, and to really design your store and build it out so that it looks nice, you don't want to rush things. There's no point in rushing this. Let's say you have a goal of becoming a millionaire, it doesn't really matter if you become a millionaire in one year or in six months or in three months, it doesn't matter, at the end of the day you're still a millionaire.

You have to understand that success is all about having the confidence and the persistence and the tenacity to actually make things work. So even though you will not make a sale in the first 14 days free trial, what matters is that you've tried and if you keep trying, then you're bound to succeed. You can only fail if you give up. If you don't give up, you're bound to succeed. Everything in my life changed when I heard the quote that 99% of people give up in business after three failures, so if you can last three failures, then you will be in the top 1% of people and guess what the top 1% of people in society? They're the highest earners, the most successful people. So automatically you're successful.

Tip number 3

If your product isn't selling, then you have to look at your weakest link. Your funnel is only as good as your weakest link. If you want to find out why your product isn't selling, try to find the weakest link and what I mean by that it can be anything on your store. It can be your price, maybe your price is too high, maybe your pictures are not good enough, maybe your sales page is just not good enough, it's not nice enough and in that case, what I recommend you do is emulate your competitors strategies and improve on them. In today's world, you can see everything that your competitors are doing and you can see exact examples of success so there no excuse for you to just basically give up.

You can go and make everything work and that's what I recommend you do if you're not selling, just do everything you can before moving on to the next store, be honest with yourself and you can always change the product. It's not the end of the world. Every single failure is a lesson. And actually, failure is better than success in a way because it teaches you something. Success doesn't teach you anything, you're just successful and that's it. That's awesome you can build on it, but it doesn't really teach you much. that's why I recommend you go smooth and slow, you don't try to rush this, and what I recommend is even if you don't make your first sale in the first 14 days trial just sign up for the plan it's $29 a month sign up for one month. I would say give yourself at least two months, just try for two months and you know for those of you out there who are really like dedicated three months minimum and I guarantee if you can stay there for three months you will succeed and you will have a profitable store that you can then scale to the hundreds of thousands and millions and tens of millions. And also keep yourself updated, never stop learning, millionaires never stop learning and that's why they're where there are in life so what I recommend you do is watch free content on YouTube and Google there's a lot of great content out there.

See you at the top!

Resources

How to set up Shopify store step by step

https://www.youtube.com/watch?v=B2h611DKbew

Facebook Ads Shopify Tutorial - E-commerce Facebook Ads Step By Step Tutorial

https://www.youtube.com/watch?v=xHo6W8k5GXs

About the Author

Brian is a Digital Marketing Manager 9-5, and an e-commerce side hustler (Dropshipping, Print on Demand & Affiliate Marketing). He focuses on helping coaches, trainer, speakers and entrepreneurs leverage & maximize every ounce of online marketing through funnels, automation & conversion techniques so they can actually ENJOY FREEDOM (which is why they became entrepreneurs in the first place Brian's mission is to empower entrepreneurs with the knowledge and tools to build radically successful businesses in creative, techy ways – so they can make a major impact while increasing their profitability in a major way.

www.ingramcontent.com/pod-product-compliance
Lightning Source LLC
Chambersburg PA
CBHW071412210526
45465CB00001B/352